FRIEND OF SINNERS

FRIEND OF SINNERS

Why Jesus cares more about
relationship than perfection

STUDY GUIDE | FIVE SESSIONS

RICH WILKERSON, JR.
WITH JUSTIN JAQUITH

NELSON
BOOKS

An Imprint of Thomas Nelson

CONTENTS

INTRODUCTION

I love having friends. That sounds pretty basic—I mean, who doesn't want friends? But think about it for a second. Friends are amazing. They support you. They laugh with you (or maybe at you; it's hard to tell sometimes). They believe in you. They tell you when your haircut looks terrible. They hack your phone. They cheer you up when you're sad. They help you survive awkward parties. Friends are so important that most of us couldn't imagine life without them.

Have you ever stopped to wonder why we care so much about having friends? I think friends are important to us because *friends are important to God*. God wants friends. And even more than that, God is a friend. He invented the whole idea of friendship, after all. And since he is perfectly selfless and the personification of love, it goes without saying that he is the best friend imaginable.

In my experience—first as a Christian and second as a pastor—many people don't see themselves as friends of Jesus. They look at Jesus as Savior, Lord, King, and God, but they don't dare to classify themselves as friends. That sounds too informal, too presumptuous. I know we sometimes sing that old song, "What a Friend We Have in Jesus." But do we really see ourselves as his friends?

Let me take it a step further. Can we believe that Jesus is a friend of *sinners*? Because again, in my experience, our mistakes always seem to throw a monkey wrench in this whole friendship-with-God thing. Maybe we can believe we are God's friends when we are living relatively holy lives: when we pray every day, go to church on Sundays, don't have any major addictions, and haven't yelled at our kids in a few days. In those moments, we might dare believe God wants to hang out with us.

But what about when we mess up? What about when we fall back into a temptation or addiction we've promised God a thousand times we would leave behind? I know how I tend to react in those moments—I subconsciously assume I just blew any chance at friendship with Jesus. He'll continue to love me . . . because he has to. But he certainly won't *want* to be my friend.

But in the last couple of years, I've come to see Jesus as more than Savior, King, and God. I've come to see him as my friend, even when I don't deserve it (which is all the time!). Actually, I've come to see him as a friend of sinners everywhere. We are all sinners, after all. Who can claim to be perfect? Nobody. Yet the Bible reveals a Jesus who actively, intentionally, and continually sought out sinners. He spent time with the people society reviled and rejected. He risked his reputation because he cared about people, not appearance.

That's why I wrote the book *Friend of Sinners*. First, because we need to believe we are God's friends, even though we are all sinners; and second, because we must realize God's friendship extends to people who are far "worse" than we are. Better and worse are such superficial terms, of course. We are all sinners in need of grace; and in Jesus, we all find the grace and friendship we need.

During the next few weeks, I pray that friendship with Jesus becomes a reality to you. I believe God wants to show you how he sees you, and he wants to affirm his commitment and love for you. You can trust him and depend on him. You can enjoy his love. Jesus is your friend, a true friend, one who "sticks closer than a brother" (Proverbs 18:24).

I also pray that as you glimpse the incomprehensible greatness of God's love for the world, you would discover a passion to befriend lost people as well. That is the natural result of friendship with Jesus. As you see the world through his eyes, you'll see people differently. They aren't good or bad, they aren't sinner or saint; they are simply children of God.

I am so grateful for your willingness to follow Jesus. Thank you for taking the time over the next five weeks to open your heart and allow him to speak to you. He has great things in store for you! There is no more exciting, fulfilling life than knowing Jesus, the friend of sinners.

—Rich Wilkerson, Jr.

HOW TO USE THIS GUIDE

The goal of this video curriculum and the accompanying study guide is to help you grow closer to Jesus and to experience friendship with him like never before. The curriculum is designed to be experienced in a small-group setting such as a home Bible study or Sunday School class. There is a unique dynamic when you learn in the context of a small group. Ultimately, the idea is not to just gain knowledge but to experience life transformation, grow in relationship with others, and apply what you learn to your day-to-day life. And what better way to learn about Jesus as your friend than surrounded by other friends?

Each participant should have his or her own copy of the study guide, as you will receive much more from this journey if you are able to reflect on the topics during the week. It is also helpful (but not essential) to obtain a copy of the *Friend of Sinners* book. The videos and material in this study guide are based on the original book, which develops more fully many of the ideas that are briefly mentioned here.

This study guide is divided into five sections, one for each week of the curriculum. Every section contains video teaching notes, group discussion questions, prayer suggestions, and recommended readings from the *Friend of Sinners* book. As a group, you will watch the video and then use the video notes and questions to engage with the topic. There is complete freedom to decide how best to use these elements to meet the needs of the group. Again, the goal is developing relationships and experiencing life change, not just "covering the material." You are encouraged to explore each topic as a group and discover what God is saying.

These times together as a group can be rewarding, refreshing, even life-changing. Things might feel a little forced or awkward at first, but don't worry. The other members of your group will soon become trusted companions. There is something about praying and learning together that is incredibly healthy for the human soul.

It is important to maintain a positive, safe environment in the group. Everyone should have an opportunity to share what they are learning to the extent they feel comfortable. Don't feel obligated to participate, but please don't keep silent if you have something that contributes to the discussion. People need to hear what you have to say!

On the other hand, no one should dominate the conversation or impose their beliefs on others. The group discussion time is a conversation, not a monologue or a debate, and differing views are welcome. People are encouraged to share their emotions, challenges, and struggles honestly, without fear of rejection or ridicule. And, of course, it is especially important to maintain confidentiality regarding what is shared.

At the end of each of the five sessions, there are three optional between-sessions activities for use during the week. These are individual, devotional activities, so feel free to use any or all of them to apply what you are learning to your daily life. You can spend as little or as much time on them as you'd like, of course, but they will typically take about twenty minutes.

Keep in mind there are no right or wrong answers—the goal is simply to engage with the topic on a personal level. You won't be required to divulge what you write, but you might find that you want to share some things with the rest of the group. Often that is the best way to learn and grow, and you might be surprised how helpful your thoughts are to others. If you have a busy week and can't get to any of the activities, don't worry! That is life sometimes. They aren't required, and you are always welcome at the group meetings.

Finally, expect God to speak to you! It's not a coincidence or accident that you have chosen to participate in this five-week journey. God has great things in store for you. He will reveal himself to you and speak to you in ways you might not even expect. Over the next few weeks, take time to pray and meditate on the things God is saying to you. You might even want to write them down for future reference. This is the beginning of a deeper relationship with Jesus, and your life will never be the same!

Note: *If you are a group leader, there are additional instructions and resources provided in the back of this guide to help you lead your members through the study.*

MISSED MESSAGE

While Jesus was having dinner at Matthew's house, many tax collectors and sinners came and ate with him and his disciples. When the Pharisees saw this, they asked his disciples, "Why does your teacher eat with tax collectors and sinners?" On hearing this, Jesus said, "It is not the healthy who need a doctor, but the sick. But go and learn what this means: 'I desire mercy, not sacrifice.' For I have not come to call the righteous, but sinners."

MATTHEW 9:10-13

Opening Thoughts

Have you ever missed the point of a rhetorical question? You genuinely thought the person wanted answers, but he or she was actually trying to send you a message. And when you, oblivious and innocent, offered your opinion, you only made things worse.

Nowhere is this clearer than in marriage. I wish someone would have sat me down prior to getting married and said, "Rich, your wife is going to ask you questions sometimes, but she won't be looking for information. Don't answer those questions, Rich. Trust me on this. Don't answer those questions!"

I had to learn this the hard way. For example, if DawnChéré says, "Why is there a wet towel in the corner of the closet?" she isn't really asking why it's there. She doesn't want me to explain the thought process behind leaving a towel to mildew in our closet, no matter how convinced I might be that my lack of showering etiquette was justified.

"Well, you see, babe, I was in a hurry, and I wasn't thinking about towels, I was thinking about Jesus and God and people and church . . ."

She'll interrupt me mid-explanation, because I'm missing the message she's trying to communicate. There is only one appropriate response: "I did it, I'm sorry, and I'll never do it again." Gentlemen, memorize those words. They could save your life.

To be fair, I ask rhetorical questions too. Except my wife is mostly perfect, so my pointed questions aren't pointed at her but at the universe in general.

"What is up with the traffic today? This is ridiculous!" I'll say. But I don't really want an answer. If you are ever my copilot, don't respond to that question by explaining local traffic patterns. I'm just going to get mad. And definitely don't tell me traffic wouldn't be an issue if we had left on time. I'll probably make you get out of the car and walk. I don't want answers. I want pity, I want empathy, and I want you to be as indignant as I am.

Missing the message is never a good thing. Not in marriage, not in friendship, and certainly not when it comes to God. Now, I'm not saying God communicates his message to us via rhetorical questions (although there are a few of those in the Bible). God has expressed himself to us very clearly through the Bible.

The problem is, we humans tend to be a little hard to communicate with sometimes. We can get so distracted, so busy, so flustered, so guilty, so self-righteous, or so set in our ways that we don't accurately interpret what the Bible says. I've done this many times, and maybe you have too. We tend to look at God through the lens of our own experience. We assume God has a certain attitude toward us because that's the attitude we would have if we were God. Or maybe we think he will react to our failure a particular way because that's how an authority figure in our lives would have reacted.

That's why Jesus came and lived among us. He wanted to show us—in living color—God's heart for humanity. Think about it for a moment. He didn't have to hang out with messy, broken, hurting humans. He could have lived in a hermit's hut on a hillside somewhere, preached a few good sermons from a distance, and died for our sins. But instead, he spent three and a half years walking, talking, teaching, preaching, laughing, healing, forgiving, guiding, praying, pleading, correcting, calling, and comforting people just like you and me. Why? So we could get the message. So we could understand what God is trying to tell us.

What is that message? *That God is a friend of sinners.* That's what the idea of "grace" means. We don't deserve God's love, because we have all failed him. But he seeks us out, he calls us to himself, and he covers our sins with his righteousness.

Jesus' relationship with Matthew the tax collector is a clear example of this (see Matthew 9:9–13). Keep in mind that tax collectors in that day were considered traitors and thieves. They took money from their fellow Jewish citizens and turned it over to the hated Roman empire. And they collected quite a bit extra for themselves as well.

Jesus found Matthew seated at his tax booth. That means he was doing exactly what had made him infamous in the first place: selling out his countrymen to make a quick buck. Jesus said, "Follow me." And Matthew got up and followed him. Just like that, he became a disciple of Jesus.

Notice what Jesus did *not* do. He didn't rebuke Matthew publicly. He didn't force him to give all the money back he had stolen. He didn't put him on a lower level than the other disciples. He didn't make him promise to never steal again. He simply showed Matthew grace and invited him to become his follower.

If we think Jesus came to bring about behavior modification, we have missed the message. His top priority in life is not to get us to stop using bad words. It's not to convince us to give our money to people in need. It's not even to fix our marriages or restore our families. Those things are good, and if you follow Jesus, you'll notice improvement in your character, your thought life, and your actions. But behavioral change is not the point.

The point is relationship. Jesus is befriending us. He is calling us to himself, and his grace has made friendship possible. No matter who we are or how badly we've messed up, grace, forgiveness, and love are available in Jesus.

Video Teaching Notes

Here are a few key points to note as you watch this week's video. Use the space provided to write down any observations or applications that come to mind as you watch.

If you miss the message of Jesus, you can find yourself in the wrong place and space in your faith journey and relationship to others.

The message of Jesus is much more than good versus bad. Jesus didn't come to make bad people good. He came to make *dead people alive*.

The story of Matthew (Levi) the tax collector in Matthew 9 is a clear illustration that Jesus is a friend of sinners. Matthew was a traitor and a thief, yet Jesus befriended him and called him.

Jesus came for everyone, but he can only save those who acknowledge their need for salvation. This includes both the obvious sinners and the self-righteous (like the Pharisees).

When we enter a relationship with Jesus, a transformation begins on the inside that eventually affects our outside life.

Many people reduce Jesus' message to a morality lesson. That is what the rich young ruler in Mark 10 did. He called Jesus "good," as if he were only a rabbi, and asked for a list of laws to keep in order to have eternal life.

It's not about what we do but about what he's done. It's about receiving his grace and living in faith. Religion makes us proud of ourselves. Grace makes us proud of Jesus.

Jesus isn't just a good teacher; he's the Savior of the world. He deserves much more than our morality, church attendance, rituals, and customs. He deserves our lives.

Group Discussion

Take a few minutes with your group members to discuss what you just watched and explore these concepts in Scripture.

1. How would you describe the message of Jesus? What was the main thing he came to teach and demonstrate?

2. How does the story of Matthew the tax collector illustrate that with Jesus, we can *belong* before we *believe*?

3. How do you think the Pharisees would have compared themselves to the tax collectors and sinners? Do you think God shared that opinion? What does their question about Jesus being a friend of sinners reveal about their attitude toward those who did not meet their standards?

4. The rich young ruler viewed Jesus as a "good teacher" and asked him, "What must I do to inherit eternal life?" (Mark 10:17 NLT). What was the problem with this approach to Jesus and his message?

5. Why do you think people so often reduce Jesus' message to mere behavior modification? Why is that underestimating the message?

6. How has Jesus' message of grace and friendship changed you personally?

Closing Prayer

Close your time together in prayer. Here are a few ideas of what you could pray about based on the topic of this session:

- Thank God for the gift of salvation through Jesus.
- Acknowledge Jesus' incredible gift of acceptance and friendship to you.
- Pray for a clearer understanding of his grace in your life.
- Invite Jesus to be Lord of your entire life, not just your behavior.
- Ask him to help you show grace and acceptance to others around you.

Recommended Reading

Review chapters 1 and 2 in the book *Friend of Sinners*. Use the space provided to write down any key points or questions you want to bring to the next group meeting. If you'd like to read ahead for the following week, read chapters 3 and 4.

PERSONAL STUDY

The following pages provide an opportunity for you to reflect personally on the topics you covered this week in the *Friend of Sinners* video and discussion. Feel free to engage with any or all of these three activities during the week. There are no right or wrong answers, and no one will see your responses unless you choose to share them. These moments alone with God are a time to allow his love, peace, and wisdom to fill your heart and mind.

The Message Matters

Missing the message another person is trying to communicate is never a good thing. That's why we try so hard to understand what other people are saying—especially when a relationship is important to us. The same holds true with Jesus. It's vital we understand what his life and teachings are meant to communicate.

1. Jesus' message can be summed up in the word *grace*. That's not an easy word to define, though, because it is such a beautiful, all-encompassing term. What does grace mean to you?

2. In Romans 3:23–24, Paul writes, "*For everyone has sinned; we all fall short of God's glorious standard. Yet God, in his grace, freely makes us right in his sight. He did this through Christ Jesus when he freed us*

from the penalty for our sins" (NLT). According to this passage, what does it mean that you are saved by grace?

3. In Luke 19:10, Jesus says, *"For the Son of Man came to seek and save those who are lost"* (NLT). What are some of the ways Jesus sought to fulfill this mission?

4. Take a few moments to write down a brief prayer of gratitude for the difference Jesus' grace has made in your life.

Unfortunately, many people who consider themselves Christians and follow-ers of Jesus . . . try to *correct* people before they *connect* with people. Not Jesus. As you read about his life and listen to his teachings, you see time and time again a man who went out of his way to befriend people who had been ostracized, labeled, and rejected by society. . . . They were friends of Jesus, and their lives were inevitably and irrevocably changed as a result.

—*FRIEND OF SINNERS*, PAGE XIII

Leveling the Playing Field

The beautiful thing about grace is that it works the same for everyone. It levels the playing field, so to speak. None of us can claim to be perfect, so we all need to *receive* grace. And those around us are also imperfect human beings, so we all need to *show* grace. Can you imagine what the world would look like if we kept those two things in mind? There would be no room for judgment, selfishness, insecurity, or comparison. Instead, we would be able celebrate God's acceptance of us and extend that acceptance to others.

1. Are there areas of your life where you need help? Where do you need God's grace in your life?

2. Is it hard for you to admit you need help, either from God or from others? Why or why not?

3. In Luke 18:10–14, Jesus told this story to those who had confidence in their righteousness and scorned others around them:

    Then Jesus told this story to some who had great confidence in their own righteousness and scorned everyone else: "Two men went to the Temple to pray. One was a Pharisee, and the other was a despised tax collector. The Pharisee stood by himself and prayed this prayer: 'I thank you, God, that I am not like other people—cheaters, sinners, adulterers. I'm certainly not like that tax collector! I fast twice a week, and I give you a tenth of my income.'

"But the tax collector stood at a distance and dared not even lift his eyes to heaven as he prayed. Instead, he beat his chest in sorrow, saying, 'O God, be merciful to me, for I am a sinner.' I tell you, this sinner, not the Pharisee, returned home justified before God. For those who exalt themselves will be humbled, and those who humble themselves will be exalted" (NLT).

What does this say about the attitude God values in us?

Who did the Pharisee trust in for his righteousness? Who did the tax collector trust in?

4. Are there people in your life to whom you have trouble showing grace and mercy? What makes it difficult to show grace to these people?

5. Do you tend to compare yourself to those around you? What are some negative effects of comparison?

Jesus' message was *grace*. It was salvation for all who believe in him. It was mercy and compassion and forgiveness for all who would put their faith in him. And I'll go even further. Jesus was the personification and the embodiment of grace. In other words, Jesus *himself* is the message. Jesus is the purpose and the point. The message isn't mere dogma or doctrine. It isn't behavioral change. The message is that no matter who you are or how badly you've messed up, grace and forgiveness are available in Jesus.

—*FRIEND OF SINNERS*, PAGE 14

Good or God

Like the rich young leader in Mark 10:17–22, sometimes we might think our walk with God is primarily about behavior, and if we do enough good things, we can gain God's acceptance. We reduce Jesus' message to a self-help program, and in so doing, we underestimate what he came to do. Remember, Jesus didn't come to help good people get better. He came to bring spiritually dead people back to life.

1. Why do you think people so often focus on behavior when they think about religion, God, or spirituality?

2. Paul writes the following in Ephesians 2:4–10:

    But because of his great love for us, God, who is rich in mercy, made us alive with Christ even when we were dead in transgressions—it is by grace you have been saved. And God raised us up with Christ and seated us with him in the heavenly realms in Christ Jesus, in order that in the coming ages he might show the incomparable riches of his grace, expressed in his kindness to us in Christ Jesus. For it is by grace you have been saved, through faith—and this is not from yourselves, it is the gift of God—not by works, so that no one can boast. For we are God's handiwork, created in Christ Jesus to do good works, which God prepared in advance for us to do.

Why isn't it possible to be "good enough" to please God on our own? What does this passage say about grace?

3. Think about how you tend to relate to God. Is it more about fear or trust? Is it more about rules or rest? Is it more about behavior or friendship? Explain.

4. Why do you think you relate to God this way? Have any authority figures in your past or present affected your view of God? Explain.

Take a few moments and ask God to reset your view of him. If you'd like, you can pray something like this:

> *Jesus, thank you for accepting me by grace. I don't trust in my own goodness or my own efforts. I have faith in you. I believe you died for my sins and rose again, and now I can have friendship with God. Help me keep my focus on you, not on myself. Help me know and believe how much you love me. I pray this in your name, amen.*

If we approach Jesus simply as a teacher, he will give us the law. But if we approach him as our Savior, he will give us grace. . . . When we underestimate Jesus, it usually has nothing to do with whether we think he can heal or provide for us. We don't underestimate his power. We underestimate his grace. We think—just like the rich young ruler—that he came to make us better. Jesus is not a self-help message. Jesus is a "he did all the work because you couldn't" message.
—*FRIEND OF SINNERS*, PAGES 37-38

SESSION TWO

WEIGHT SHIFT

"Come to me, all you who are weary and burdened, and I will
give you rest. Take my yoke upon you and learn from me, for I am
gentle and humble in heart, and you will find rest for your souls.
For my yoke is easy and my burden is light."

MATTHEW 11:28-30

Opening Thoughts

Have you ever had a small child offer to help you unload the car, make a meal, or carry a heavy object? The ensuing experience always involves a lot of enthusiasm but very little efficiency. During the whole process, you are aware you could accomplish the task a lot easier on your own. But where's the fun in that?

I'm pretty sure God looks at our "help" the same way. It's cute, it's noble, it's awww-inspiring, and it's a little bit laughable, all at the same time. Remember, God spoke worlds into existence in a matter of days. He invented time, gravity, and light. He doesn't just understand quantum physics—he created it. He clearly is not dependent on our energy, our efforts, or our plans. And yet, he loves to involve us in the process. He puts real responsibility in our hands, and he lets us make a lot of decisions. Even though he is sovereign, he invites us to help him.

The problem, though, is that sometimes we think we are doing it all on our own. We forget that he is carrying the bulk of the load. We develop a lifestyle of being stressed out, overwhelmed, and over-burdened. That is not the life God created us to lead. Just as our physical bodies can be harmed by carrying too much weight, so our inner selves—our thoughts, our emotions, our decisions—can be hurt if we carry burdens that only God can carry.

Jesus was referring to this in Matthew 11:28–30, when he told the people in the large crowd that had gathered to come to him, and he would give them rest. If we find ourselves worn out and stressed out, maybe the problem isn't that God is asking too much, but that we are insisting on carrying too much. God wants to carry the weight that is too heavy for us.

Nowhere is this clearer than in how God deals with our sin. The word *sin* refers to the things in our lives that don't measure up to the standard of righteousness and holiness that God created us to enjoy. Sin is the greatest weight of all. Sin separates from God, hurts our lives, affects our relationships with others, and brings us under a cloud of guilt and shame. On our own, we could never carry the weight of sin.

So Jesus carried it for us. It's that simple. Jesus bore our guilt, our punishment, and our condemnation on the cross. As Paul wrote, "God made him who had no sin to be sin for us, so that in him we might become the righteousness of God" (2 Corinthians 5:21). Jesus isn't a taskmaster, a judge, or a boss. He's a friend, and he carries the weight we could never bear.

The difference between religion and grace is that religion is about doing, while grace is about resting in what is already done. The more we come to know Jesus as the friend of sinners, the more we will be able to find true rest for our souls.

God already knows our failures, and he isn't intimidated or disgusted or embarrassed by them. Instead of attempting to hide our weaknesses from him or overcome them on our own, we can simply lean on his strength in every area of our lives. His strength becomes our strength. His righteousness becomes our righteousness. His rest becomes our rest.

Video Teaching Notes

Here are a few key points to note as you watch this week's video. Use the space provided to write down any observations or applications that come to mind as you watch.

Jesus isn't just our Savior; he's our sustainer. He didn't just come to visit us but to walk with us and to help us.

We tend to carry weight we shouldn't carry. This includes the weight of the performance of yesterday, the pressures of today, and the worries of tomorrow.

In Matthew 11:28–30, Jesus tells us if we are carrying too much, we can come to him. That is the message of the friend of sinners: we can come just as we are, and he will give us true rest.

Jesus invites us to take his yoke upon us. When we yoke our lives to Jesus, we tap into his supernatural power. His effort becomes our effort; his work becomes our work.

Jesus is our friend. He is always with us, and he won't let the weight of life crush us.

We have real responsibility, but we can cast our cares on Jesus. He cares for us, and he will care for the things that concern us.

The story of Zacchaeus in Luke 19 shows how much humanity needs Jesus' message of grace. It also shows how one encounter with Jesus led to amazing generosity and genuine conversion.

Jesus takes the initiative to find lost people and give them hope. He came to seek us, save us, walk with us, and help us.

Group Discussion

Take a few minutes with your group members to discuss what you just watched and explore these concepts in Scripture.

1. We all know that carrying too much physical weight can harm our bodies. What are the negative results when our souls carry too much weight for too long?

2. Think about yesterday's performance, today's pressures, and tomorrow's worries. What are some weights you regularly find yourself carrying that are too heavy to carry alone?

3. What does it mean to take Jesus' yoke upon you (see Matthew 11:28–30)?

4. Jesus said his yoke is easy and his burden is light. How does connecting yourself to Jesus make your burdens lighter than before?

5. The Bible encourages us to cast all our care upon the Lord because he cares for us (see 1 Peter 5:7). What are some practical ways to "cast" those worries on God?

6. One encounter with Jesus led to dramatic changes in Zacchaeus' life. How have you seen your life change since you began following Jesus?

Closing Prayer

Close your time together in prayer. Here are a few ideas of what you could pray about based on the topic of this session:

- Thank Jesus for helping you carry the weights and pressures of life.
- Thank him that your past, present, and future burdens are in his hands.
- Ask Jesus to help you walk closely with him and to rest in his strength.
- Declare that you trust Jesus to care for you, and allow him to take your cares.
- Pray that as you walk with Jesus, he would bring about life transformation.

Recommended Reading

Review chapters 3 and 4 in the book *Friend of Sinners*. Use the space provided to write down any key points or questions you want to bring to the next group meeting. If you'd like to read ahead for the following week, read chapters 5 through 7.

PERSONAL STUDY

The following pages provide an opportunity for you to reflect personally on the topics you covered this week in the *Friend of Sinners* video and discussion. Feel free to engage with any or all of these three activities during the week. There are no right or wrong answers, and no one will see your responses unless you choose to share them. These moments alone with God are a time to allow his love, peace, and wisdom to fill your heart and mind.

Shifting the Weight

When it comes to our souls, we can be carrying heavy burdens without even realizing it. Our culture, experience, and upbringing often teach us that we have to do things on our own. We are told to be strong, to figure things out, to fight for what we want. While strength and hard work are important, we were never intended to face life alone. Jesus wants to help us carry the burdens of life. When we shift our weight onto him, we find rest for our souls.

1. Under each category, write down situations or areas where you sometimes find yourself carrying too much weight.

   Performance of yesterday (guilt or shame for past failures, circumstances, mistakes, or abuse)

Pressures of today (difficulties that are occupying your mind and emotions right now)

Worries of tomorrow (risks, fears, or uncertainties that might lie ahead of you)

2. Looking at the list above, do you notice any patterns? Are there specific areas of life where you tend to have trouble trusting and resting in Jesus?

3. What are some practical things you could do to develop faith and trust in these areas?

4. What positive results do you expect to see in your life from learning to let Jesus carry the weight you cannot carry?

Jesus is not just the Savior—he's the sustainer. He's not just the author of our faith—he's the finisher, the one who perfects and completes and carries our faith through to the end. The more we come to know Jesus as the friend of sinners, the more we will be able to truly find rest for our souls.

—*FRIEND OF SINNERS,* PAGE 46

Jesus Is Bigger

What is Jesus' message? Grace. Who is it for? Sinners. That pretty much sums up why Jesus came to earth. And, by the way, we are *all* sinners, so we can *all* receive his grace. He doesn't expect perfection. Our mistakes don't drive us away from him—they bring us closer to him. Jesus' grace is big enough to handle our sins, our defects, and our weaknesses. It's bigger than our fears. It's bigger than our dumb decisions. It's bigger than our wrong opinions about ourselves. It's bigger than the labels other people put on us. No matter who we are, what we've done, or how big our need, Jesus' grace is there for us.

1. Make a list of the things that most frustrate you about yourself or about your circumstances, and then circle the three most important ones.

    Why do these areas frustrate you so much?

2. How do you usually try to deal with these frustrating areas? Do your reactions reflect a trust in Jesus, or is possible you are carrying burdens he wants to carry for you?

3. In Psalm 103:13–14, David writes, *"As a father has compassion on his children, so the LORD has compassion on his faithful followers. For he knows what we are made of; he realizes we are made of clay"* (NET).What does this passage tell you about how God deals with your weaknesses?

4. The writer of Hebrews states, *"Let us then approach God's throne of grace with confidence, so that we may receive mercy and find grace to help us in our time of need"* (4:16). What kind of attitude and approach should you have when you talk to God about your needs?

Taking [Jesus'] yoke upon us isn't about pulling more weight. It's about letting him pull our weight. He will carry what we could never carry. When we harness ourselves to him—to his grace, his power, his sufficiency—everything changes. We will accomplish things we never thought possible, because we are yoked to the supernatural power of Jesus.

—*FRIEND OF SINNERS,* PAGES 52–53

Grace Isn't Fair

Justice is a funny thing. We all say we are in favor of fairness, of justice, of being held responsible for our actions. We agree that these are universal concepts and that we should strive to have a fair and just world. But when we have failed, we come face to face with our need for grace, for mercy, for a second chance. When justice becomes our accuser, we need a Savior and an advocate. That's what Jesus does. As the friend of sinners, he shows us undeserved grace, unearned mercy, and unconditional love.

1. Reread the story of Zacchaeus in Luke 19:1–10. Try to imagine the reaction of the townspeople (especially the Pharisees) when Jesus chose Zacchaeus' house to visit. What do you think they were thinking?

2. Do you tend to be quick to judge other people's mistakes, or do you give them the benefit of the doubt? Are there certain people or groups of people you judge more quickly? Explain.

3. Can you think of a time in your life when you were shown mercy and grace by someone? Maybe a boss at work, or a forgiving spouse, or a teacher at school?

4. What effect has grace had on your life? How is mercy often more powerful and effective than strict justice?

5. Write down the names of two or three people you know who could use some extra (and undeserved) grace. What are practical ways you could show them unconditional love in the next few days?

Take a few moments and ask God to help you trust him and rest in his grace. If you'd like, you can pray something like this:

God, thank you for carrying the weight I could never carry. Help me trust you, rest in you, and believe in you, especially when I'm facing things that are too big for me. I know you are faithful. You will lead me and protect me no matter what life might bring my way. Teach me to show your mercy and grace to those around me, just as you have shown me mercy and grace. I pray this in Jesus' name, amen.

Jesus didn't come to give you what you deserve. He came to give you what *he* deserves. He is your "fast pass." His grace is the reason you can have peace with God and with yourself. You can skip the never-ending lines of legalism, self-effort, and dead works when you have Jesus. He already found you. He already picked you. He already called your name. Now he's standing at the door of your heart, waiting to be your friend. You just have to open the door.

—*FRIEND OF SINNERS,* PAGE 79

SESSION THREE

LOST AND FOUND

"The father said to his servants, 'Quick! Bring the best robe and
put it on him. Put a ring on his finger and sandals on his feet.
Bring the fattened calf and kill it. Let's have a feast and
celebrate. For this son of mine was dead and is alive again;
he was lost and is found.' So they began to celebrate."

LUKE 15:22-24

Opening Thoughts

Have you ever lost something important? I lose things on a regular basis. It's slightly embarrassing, actually. Some people might call me distracted, but I prefer to think of myself as being very . . . present.

I'm an in-the-moment kind of guy. That means that whatever I'm doing right now is the most important thing in the world, and everything else is forgotten. Including the location of my wallet, my keys, my laptop, my sunglasses, my wife, or my dignity.

If you've ever lost something of value to you, then you are familiar with the passion and purpose that possess you the instant you realize your loss. Suddenly you can think of nothing else but finding what you lost. And when you do find it, you celebrate shamelessly. When something that is lost is found, a party should follow. That's human nature.

I think it's God's nature, too. The Bible shows us a God who is obsessed with finding lost things. Specifically, he is obsessed with lost *people*. People are his passion, his pride, and his purpose. There is nothing that makes God happier than lost people returning home.

In Luke 15, Jesus described the party that happens in heaven when lost people come home. In three short stories, or parables, Jesus illustrated the desperation of losing something of value and the celebration that accompanies finding it again. He said, "There is more joy in heaven over one lost sinner who repents and returns to God than over ninety-nine others who are righteous and haven't strayed away!" (verse 7 NLT).

These three stories were Jesus' explanation of his mission on earth. Why did he have to defend his mission? Because Jesus was often accused by religious leaders of spending too much time with bad people. "He's a friend of sinners," they said (Luke 7:34). They meant those words as a mark of shame, but Jesus took it as a badge of honor. That was exactly who he was and what he wanted to do: find, befriend, serve, and save lost people.

There were two groups of people listening to him that day. Some were considered bad people (tax collectors and other "sinners") and some were considered good people (Pharisees and other religious leaders). While all three parables illustrated the value God places on lost things, the third one, about the prodigal son and the judgmental older brother, specifically addressed these two groups of people. It leveled the playing field for both. Jesus showed them that God's grace extends to both sinner and saint. Ultimately, we are all equally loved by the Father and equally in need of his grace. None of us should look down on another.

When we experience God's grace, two things happen. First, we realize our value in God's eyes. And second, we realize everyone else's value in God's eyes. There is something about grace that enables us and motivates us to share God's love with other people. Our calling and our commission are not to just discover Jesus' love for ourselves but to share it with others.

People everywhere are looking for God. They might not describe themselves that way, because God has often been presented in such a negative light. The last thing many lost people think they need is "religion." In their minds, they are just looking for happiness, for peace, for fulfillment; but in reality, those things are only found in the arms of the Father. If we can show people that Jesus is a friend of sinners, if we can help them discover the grace, acceptance, love, and loyalty that God has for humanity, their lives will be changed forever.

Maybe you are still deciding what you believe about Jesus, and you aren't sure you even need to be "found" or "saved." Or maybe you are a follower of Jesus and have begun to experience the joy, peace, and rest that come from being safe in his love. Either way, God is passionate about you. He loves us all alike, and he wants the best for each of us.

Video Teaching Notes

Here are a few key points to note as you watch this week's video. Use the space provided to write down any observations or applications that come to mind as you watch.

Jesus was often accused of being a friend of sinners. The three stories he told in Luke 15:1–32 were his explanation and defense.

The first story was about a shepherd leaving ninety-nine sheep behind in search of one lost sheep. This story illustrates how obsessed God is with finding lost things.

The second story was about a woman with ten coins who lost one and turned her house upside down until she found it. This story shows the value God places on every person, whether lost or found.

The third story was about two sons—one a prodigal, the other a judgmental older brother—which spoke to both groups listening to Jesus. The sinners would have identified with the prodigal son, and the Pharisees were meant to see themselves in the older brother.

Sin takes you further than you wanted to go, it makes you stay longer than you wanted to stay, and it promises something it cannot deliver.

Before the son could get to the father, the father ran toward him and embraced him. In the same way, God took the initiative to look for us, to come to us, and to accept us.

God came both for those who committed the crime and those who judge the crime. Whether we are the prodigal or the Pharisee in the story, Jesus loves us and he came for us.

Jesus' mission and ministry were about finding lost things. The cross *expressed* his passion for us. We *experience* his love and grace. Then we *evangelize*, sharing Jesus' love with the lost.

Group Discussion

Take a few minutes with your group members to discuss what you just watched and explore these concepts in Scripture.

1. In the events of Luke 15, what was the difference in attitude between the sinners and the Pharisees? How did each group see Jesus?

2. What does the parable of the shepherd leaving the ninety-nine sheep to go after the one lost sheep tell you about God's heart?

3. What does the story of the woman searching for her lost coin tell you about the value of a human soul in God's eyes?

4. In the story of the two sons, do you identify more with the younger son (the prodigal) or with the older son? Why?

5. What can you learn from the fact that the father was watching and waiting for his son—and that he ran to greet him?

6. Are you passionate about lost people? What practical things can you do this week to help lost people see the love of Jesus?

Closing Prayer

Close your time together in prayer. Here are a few ideas of what you could pray about based on the topic of this session:

- Thank God for his passion for lost people—including you.
- Pray for a greater revelation of God's love and acceptance for you, even when you stray.
- Ask God to help you value people the way he does.
- Pray for a heart of compassion and grace toward lost people.
- Ask God to increase your passion for the lost and hurting around you.
- Pray for specific opportunities to show Jesus' love and grace to other people this week.

Recommended Reading

Review chapters 5 through 7 in the book *Friend of Sinners*. Use the space provided to write down any key points or questions you want to bring to the next group meeting. If you'd like to read ahead for the following week, read chapters 8 and 9.

PERSONAL STUDY

The following pages provide an opportunity for you to reflect personally on the topics you covered this week in the *Friend of Sinners* video and discussion. Feel free to engage with any or all of these three activities during the week. There are no right or wrong answers, and no one will see your responses unless you choose to share them. These moments alone with God are a time to allow his love, peace, and wisdom to fill your heart and mind.

Lost and Found

Sometimes you don't know how much you care about something until you lose it. It could be something material, like a coat or a jewelry item; or it could be something immaterial but even more significant, like a relationship. When it's gone, suddenly you realize just how much it meant to you. Just as our reactions to loss reflect the value we place on things, so God's reaction to lost people reveals his heart for every person. His desperate, focused, relentless pursuit of people demonstrates his love for humanity.

1. Think about a time you lost something important to you. How did you react? What emotions did you feel?

2. What did you do, or what would you have been willing to do, to recover what you lost?

3. What emotions do you think God feels when he sees people who are spiritually lost (separated from relationship with him)?

4. Think about a time you found something that had been lost. How does the emotion you felt compare to how God feels when lost people are found?

5. Peter writes, *"For 'you were like sheep going astray,' but now you have returned to the Shepherd and Overseer of your souls"* (1 Peter 2:25). What does this verse mean to you?

6. Why do you think Jesus came to earth? What difference has he made in your life?

God is obsessed with finding what is lost because of his overpowering love for people. Remember what Jesus told Zacchaeus? "The Son of Man came to seek and save those who are lost" (Luke 19:10 NLT). That's his mission. That's his passion. No matter who you are, what you've done, or where you find yourself, Jesus is ready to embrace you. And no matter who he brings into your path in the future, his grace is sufficient for them as well.

—*FRIEND OF SINNERS,* PAGE 101

He Knows Your Name

God doesn't just love humanity in some general, cosmic sense. He loves each and every one of us specifically. He knows our names, he knows our stories, and he knows the plans he has for our lives. Jesus demonstrated this during his time on earth by relating to individuals, often by name.

1. Time after time, Jesus sought out people who needed him and spoke directly into their lives. Below are a few examples of people whom Jesus called by name. Take a few minutes to read the story of his or her encounter with Jesus, and then answer the questions that follow.

    Martha: Read Luke 10:38–42

    • What was this person's primary need?

    • How did Jesus address the need?

- How can you apply what Jesus said to your own life?

Mary Magdalene: Read John 20:11–18
- What was this person's primary need?

- How did Jesus address the need?

- How can you apply what Jesus said to your own life?

Peter: Read John 21:1–19
- What was this person's primary need?

- How did Jesus address the need?

- How can you apply what Jesus said to your own life?

Paul, formerly Saul: Read Acts 9:1–19

- What was this person's primary need?

- How did Jesus address the need?

- How can you apply what Jesus said to your own life?

2. Read the following passage from Psalm 139:13–18:

> *You made all the delicate, inner parts of my body*
>   *and knit me together in my mother's womb.*
> *Thank you for making me so wonderfully complex!*
>   *Your workmanship is marvelous—how well I know it.*
> *You watched me as I was being formed in utter seclusion,*
>   *as I was woven together in the dark of the womb.*
> *You saw me before I was born.*
>   *Every day of my life was recorded in your book.*
> *Every moment was laid out*
>   *before a single day had passed.*
>
> *How precious are your thoughts about me, O God.*
>   *They cannot be numbered!*
> *I can't even count them;*
>   *they outnumber the grains of sand!*
> *And when I wake up,*
>   *you are still with me!* (NLT).

How much does God think about you? What does that tell you about how important you are to him?

Take a few moments to thank God for his intimate knowledge of you and his immense love for you. You mean more to him than anything else, and he thinks about you all the time. Is there anything more encouraging than that?

Jesus knows your name. . . . God is both big and small. He's so big he can help you and so small he knows every detail about you. He is big enough to be small enough to be your friend and companion throughout life. In knowing your name, he knows everything there is to know about you. He loves you. He has a plan for you. He is watching over you.

—*FRIEND OF SINNERS,* PAGE 120

Worth It

There is a fascinating story in Mark 2:1–12 of four men who wanted to help their paralyzed friend meet Jesus. They knew that if they could only get their friend to Jesus, his life would be changed forever. But there was a problem. The crowd around the house where Jesus was teaching was so thick they couldn't even get close. So they got creative. They carried the man to the roof on his stretcher, tore open a hole in the roof, and lowered the man right down to

Jesus' feet. When Jesus saw their faith, he forgave the man's sins and healed his body. It was a miracle on many levels, all because the four friends were *committed* and *creative*. In the same way, we need to be committed and creative in our approach to helping lost people.

1. How do you think Jesus' teachings, life, and message could benefit people in your life? List three or four people you know personally who might be open to hearing about Jesus' love for them.

2. Are you willing and committed to share Jesus' love with those people if God opens the door? What are some things that might hinder you from reaching out to them? How can you prepare yourself to be ready when God opens the door to share with them?

3. What creative ways could you share God's love with people in your life? Remember, the goal isn't to fulfill some quota or religious obligation, but rather to help people see Jesus for who he is. It's about *people*, not *you*. And more often than not, people see God's love through other people, not through

sermons. Brainstorm a few authentic, organic, simple ways you could show the love and grace of Jesus to others this week.

This week, ask God for help sharing his love with people who are lost. You might pray something like this:

God, thank you for finding me when I was lost. You saw me, you loved me, and you valued me, even when I was far away from you. Please give me that same love and passion for others. Help me see people the way you see them. Show me how to take the initiative to reach out to them. Open doors of opportunity so I can help hurting people find peace in you. In Jesus' name, amen.

Something powerful happens when we have faith for other people. God takes notice, and he does impossible things on their behalf. *Your* faith matters. If you are that mom praying for your boy, don't stop. If you are that grandmother, keep believing for the prodigal grandson or granddaughter. . . . Don't put people on time lines; don't stamp expiration dates on them; don't grade them "incomplete" and move on. Have faith that God can intervene even when your patience long ago ran thin.

—*FRIEND OF SINNERS*, PAGE 141

COMFORTABLY UNCOMFORTABLE

"But a Samaritan, as he traveled, came where the man was;
and when he saw him, he took pity on him. He went to him and
bandaged his wounds, pouring on oil and wine. Then he put the
man on his own donkey, brought him to an inn and took care of him.
The next day he took out two denarii and gave them to the
innkeeper. 'Look after him,' he said, 'and when I return, I will
reimburse you for any extra expense you may have.'"

LUKE 10:33-35

Opening Thoughts

There are certain sounds that just naturally make you uncomfortable. Fingernails on chalkboard, for example. Or cats fighting outside the window at night. Or loud sirens when you are stuck in rush-hour traffic and can't get out of the way.

We do our best to avoid those sounds. But there is another wince-inducing noise that is a daily occurrence for most of us. In fact, we place ourselves within range of this sound on purpose, and we invite it to make us uncomfortable each morning.

It's called the alarm clock.

I don't think I've ever met anyone who enjoys the sound of their alarm ringing in the morning. As a matter of fact, there have been times when I've been out with friends and all of a sudden, someone's iPhone alarm went off, and everyone immediately groaned out loud at the unmistakable tone.

Alarm clocks are a necessary evil—an evil we accept because we'd rather be made temporarily uncomfortable and keep our jobs than remain comfortably asleep until noon and end up unemployed. The grogginess isn't fun, but it's nothing a cup of coffee or a shower can't fix; and soon we are fully awake and ready for the activities of the day. And assuming we like our jobs and our lives in general, being awake and productive is far better than lying in bed all day.

That's called *maturity*. It's called growing up. Sooner or later, we all learn the importance of becoming comfortable with being uncomfortable. We realize that the discomfort lasts only a moment, but it's worth it to attain the results on the other side.

The same principle holds true when it comes to helping other people see Jesus. It's not always easy. Sometimes there are awkward moments. Sometimes we face rejection or misunderstanding. But the uncomfortable moments are temporary, and ultimately, it's all worth it when people discover Jesus' love.

Jesus once told a famous story to illustrate exactly this point. It's often called the parable of the Good Samaritan. Before I recap the story, I should mention the backstory. A rather self-righteous man had just told Jesus that all the law could be summed up in two commandments: love God with all your heart and love your neighbor as yourself. So far, so good. But then he asked the question everyone was thinking: "Who is my neighbor?" (Luke 10:29 NLT). The Bible says he was trying to justify himself with this question. In other words, he wanted to narrow down exactly who he needed to love so he could check that off his list and get on with his self-focused life.

Jesus replied with a parable and a question. In his story, a man on a journey was assaulted and left for dead by thieves. Two different respected religious leaders walked by without helping. Then a third man, a Samaritan, came along. Unlike the other two, he stopped to help the man. He even went so far as to put him on his donkey, carry him to an inn, and leave money for his expenses. Then Jesus said, "Now which of these three would you say was a neighbor to the man who was attacked by bandits?" (verse 36 NLT).

The answer was obvious. The Samaritan was the only one of the three who was comfortable becoming uncomfortable. Jesus wanted this man—and each of us—to stop asking, "Who is my neighbor?" and instead ask, "Who can I be a neighbor to?" In other words, let's start taking the initiative to seek and serve the lost, just as Jesus did.

Jesus himself experienced discomfort and pain, and he did it willingly, because he knew the result would be salvation for each of us. He loved us so much that he faced rejection, mockery, torture, and ultimately death. He made himself uncomfortable in order to bring us comfort. He was the ultimate Good Samaritan.

Now it's our turn. As followers of Jesus, we have the privilege, responsibility, and calling to go outside our comfort zones in order to help other people. We are called to help hurting, lost people find hope in Jesus.

Video Teaching Notes

Here are a few key points to note as you watch this week's video. Use the space provided to write down any observations or applications that come to mind as you watch.

Once we've encountered the friend of sinners, we are called to be friends to sinners. We need to learn to be comfortable with getting *uncomfortable* in order to share the gospel.

In Luke 10, a lawyer asked Jesus who his neighbor was. In the story Jesus told in response, the priest represents people who see problems, pain, and people in need and say, "It's not my problem."

The Levite represents people who say, "The problem is too big for me." However, you don't need to be qualified to help others—you just need to have had an encounter with Jesus.

The Samaritan, unlike the other two who passed by, was filled with compassion and stopped to help. He represents those who say, "I know the answer to the problem."

There are four steps to helping people: *feel* compassion, *focus* on the need, *fund* the solution, and *follow through* with what you've begun.

Jesus finishes with a question: "Who was the neighbor to the man in need?" In other words, don't ask who your neighbor is; instead, ask who you can be a neighbor to.

Jesus is the only one who can love this way. Ultimately, this story points to the friend of sinners. We were beat up by the world, sin, and law, but Jesus found us and saved us.

Our job as believers is to share freely the good news of Jesus. It's to be comfortable being uncomfortable. We can't solve problems, but we can cross the street and help those around us.

Group Discussion Questions

Take a few minutes with your group members to discuss what you just watched and explore these concepts in Scripture.

1. The word *gospel* means good news. Jesus found you in your sin, befriended you, and showed you grace. Once you have encountered Jesus' love, what should your reaction be?

2. What does it mean to be "comfortably uncomfortable" for the good news of Jesus' love?

3. The story of the Good Samaritan illustrates three different reactions to people's problems and pain. Some people say, "It's not my problem." Why do you think people react this way? Is this something you would tend to say, or do you find yourself going out of your way to help people?

4. Other people say, "The problem is too big for me." Why do you think people feel this way? How could you change your perspective of God, yourself, or the problems around you so that you can avoid becoming overwhelmed?

5. The lawyer asked Jesus this question: "Who is my neighbor?" Jesus replied with a question of his own: "Who was the neighbor to the man in need?" What is the difference between these two questions?

6. What has Jesus done for you personally? Share one or two things that you have seen change in your life since you met the friend of sinners for yourself. Does what Jesus has done for you inspire you to help others meet Jesus?

Closing Prayer

Close your time together in prayer. Here are a few ideas of what you could pray about based on the topic of this session:

- Thank Jesus for finding you and befriending you even when you didn't deserve it.
- Pray that you would become comfortable with being uncomfortable; that you would go outside your comfort zone to help others.
- Ask God to open your eyes to become aware of people's needs rather than just walking by.
- Pray for the faith and courage to bring healing to hurting people.
- Ask and believe for open doors to share Jesus' love with people in your world.

Recommended Reading

Review chapters 8 and 9 in the book *Friend of Sinners*. Use the space provided to write down any key points or questions you want to bring to the next group meeting. If you'd like to read ahead for the following week, read chapter 10 and the epilogue.

PERSONAL STUDY

The following pages provide an opportunity for you to reflect personally on the topics you covered this week in the *Friend of Sinners* video and discussion. Feel free to engage with any or all of these three activities during the week. There are no right or wrong answers, and no one will see your responses unless you choose to share them. These moments alone with God are a time to allow his love, peace, and wisdom to fill your heart and mind.

Comfort Is Overrated

Does it ever seem like we spend a lot of time and resources on being comfortable? There's nothing wrong with comfort, of course. God created life to be enjoyed. But if we are honest, comfort doesn't bring true happiness. And it certainly isn't the point of life. We were meant for bigger, better, and bolder things than just avoiding pain or inconvenience. Jesus proved that by living a life focused on people. He showed us that our lives become exponentially more significant when we invest ourselves in others.

1. Read the following words from Philippians 2:6–9:

    Though he was God,
    *   he did not think of equality with God*
    *   as something to cling to.*
    Instead, he gave up his divine privileges;
    *   he took the humble position of a slave*
    *   and was born as a human being.*

> *When he appeared in human form,*
> > *he humbled himself in obedience to God*
> > *and died a criminal's death on a cross.*
> *Therefore, God elevated him to the place of highest honor*
> > *and gave him the name above all other names* (NLT).

What does this passage tell you about Jesus' attitude toward comfort and privilege?

2. What sacrifices did Jesus make that demonstrate his commitment to us?

3. Now read these words from Hebrews 12:1–3:

> *And let us run with endurance the race God has set before us. We do this by keeping our eyes on Jesus, the champion who initiates and perfects our faith. Because of the joy awaiting him, he endured the cross, disregarding its shame. Now he is seated in the place of honor beside God's throne. Think of all the hostility he endured from sinful people; then you won't become weary and give up* (NLT).

What motivated Jesus to endure the cross?

4. What reward did Jesus receive?

5. What are some things you might have to give up or endure in order to help other people? What rewards or positive results do you think you will see if you persevere and make the sacrifices needed to serve others?

We need to get comfortable with being uncomfortable. We need to learn how to be uncomfortable while maintaining a spirit of comfort. In other words, we need to keep the flow going with God. He comforts us, heals us, guides us, and refreshes us; and we turn around and pour that out to others.

—*FRIEND OF SINNERS,* PAGE 174

The Problem and the Answer

The story of the Good Samaritan is one of the clearest illustrations of God's heart for humanity recorded in Scripture. It shows us how God responds to pain . . . and how we should respond as well. It also highlights a couple of wrong responses to people's pain. The following questions will help you evaluate your responses to people in need. As you learn to love and live like Jesus, you will discover an ever-greater passion to help others.

The Priest: *"It's not my problem."*
The priest was called, equipped, and expected to help hurting people. And yet, he seemed to be too busy to be inconvenienced by the man's need.

- What are some of the things in society and culture today that distract you from seeing or helping people?

- Can you think of a time when you were tempted to say, "That's not my problem," but you stopped to help anyway? How were you able to help? How did you feel afterward?

- Are there people in pain around you whose problems you are tempted to ignore? Write down one or two specific situations in which you feel God might be asking you to get involved. Then take some moments to pray for wisdom and open doors.

The Levite: *"The problem is too big."*
Since the Levite was only an assistant in the temple, not a priest, he might not have felt qualified. He probably looked at the man's pain and thought there was nothing he could do.

- What are some of the problems people face today that can seem overwhelming to them? Do you believe God wants to help them with those problems? Why or why not?

- Can you think of a time *you* felt overwhelmed by someone's problem? How did you respond? In retrospect, should you have done anything differently?

- Sometimes the problem isn't the problem—it's your perspective that's the problem. After all, God is big enough to meet any need. Can you think of anything that should change in your perspective of yourself, others, or God that could help you feel less overwhelmed by pain?

The Samaritan: *"I know the answer."*
The Samaritan was the least likely to help because there was a great deal of prejudice and hatred between Jews and Samaritans. And yet, he went above and beyond what anyone could have expected. He made himself uncomfortable in order to comfort, heal, and save the hurting man.

• What do you think motivated the Samaritan? How can you apply that to your own life?

• Why are we sometimes uncomfortable with helping hurting people? What are we afraid of? How does true love help us overcome those hindrances?

• The real point of this story is that Jesus is the Good Samaritan, not us. We help hurting people, but we do so by taking them to Jesus. Make a list of people in your life that need more of Jesus' love and grace. Then take a few moments to pray for them by name, asking God to help them and, if needed, to use you in the process.

Jesus posed one final question to the lawyer: "Which of these three, do you think, proved to be a neighbor to the man?" (Luke 10:36 ESV). Two thousand years later, there is still a bit of this lawyer in each of us, I'm afraid. We still look for ways to justify loving our good neighbors while ignoring our bad ones. I'm not just talking about the people who live on our block or in our apartment building. I mean those whose lives intersect ours regularly; people we always look at but never see, people who need help but are all too easy to ignore.

—*FRIEND OF SINNERS,* PAGES 152–153

How to Help

Okay, so you've decided you want to help people. You've seen what Jesus has done in your life, and you know there are people around you who desperately need that same grace and aid. What next? How can you help hurting individuals in your world? Here are four practical steps that can be applied to just about any situation.

Step 1: Feel

The Good Samaritan felt compassion for the hurting man, just as God feels compassion for hurting humanity. The first step toward helping people is always love and empathy. On a scale of 1 (low) to 10 (high), how would you rate yourself in the following areas?

I am aware of what people around me are feeling. ____

I remember what is important to my friends and take time to ask them about those things. ____

I am emotionally moved by what others are going through, whether good or bad. ____

I take time to listen to people when they express their pain and their feelings. ____

I can listen to people first, without immediately trying to "fix" them or solve their problems. ____

In conversation, my body language communicates patience and concern for people. ____

I care more about people's well-being than my schedule, efficiency, or results. ____

Step 2: Focus

Feeling is the first step, and sometimes that is all that is needed. But in many instances, you'll find that God wants you to take

practical steps to help. That means taking time to truly understand the situation at hand. Again, rate yourself in the following areas and see what things could be improved.

I notice people's specific needs or desires. ____

I wait until I get the facts before I make judgments ____
about problems I come across.

I am able to give my undivided attention to a ____
problem at hand.

I am willing to set aside my plans and my agenda ____
when I come across an urgent need.

I can look at difficult situations and determine ____
practical ways to help.

Step 3: Fund

Love always gives. That's the nature of God, and it should be
our natural reaction when we see people in need. We don't give
out of obligation, but rather out of a genuine concern for people combined with faith in God's power to meet needs—both
ours and theirs. It's a beautiful partnership that produces genuine change. Again using a scale of 1 to 10, evaluate your willingness to give the following resources. How easy is it for you
to use what you have to help others?

Time ____

Money or other material possessions ____

Energy and hard work ____

Creativity ____

Talents ____

What specific talents, abilities, or gifts do you have that you could use to help others? Is there something stopping you from using what you have to love and serve?

Step 4: Follow Through
Finally, true concern for others involves a commitment to see things through to the end. Needs might not be met overnight, and lasting healing often requires a process.

- Look back at the names you listed at the end of the section titled, "The Problem and the Answer." Are there specific people in your life who God is asking you to love and help on an ongoing basis? Who are they?

- What are their specific needs?

- For each person you wrote down above, what is one practical thing you can do this week to help him or her?

Take a few moments and ask Jesus to help you see and help people in need around you. If you'd like, you can pray something like this:

> *Jesus, thank you for being the ultimate Good Samaritan, both in my life and in the lives of those around me. You are the answer, and your heart is to help and to heal people in pain. Show me who my neighbors are—those people in my life who are hurting and in need of my assistance. Give me compassion, courage, and wisdom to help them. Guide me as I lead them to you. In your name I pray, amen.*

Yes, we should love people. Yes, God will put people in our paths we can assist. Yes, compassion will motivate us to seek and aid people in need. We have the privilege of helping people, but we don't go to a hurting world on the basis of our own goodness, our own holiness, or our own efforts. We take Jesus to a hurting world because Jesus is the good Samaritan in this story. That is what he was trying to say. The whole story was a setup to point people to him.

—*FRIEND OF SINNERS,* PAGE 160

HOW TO BE GREAT

He called a little child to him, and placed the child among them. And he said: "Truly I tell you, unless you change and become like little children, you will never enter the kingdom of heaven. Therefore, whoever takes the lowly position of this child is the greatest in the kingdom of heaven. And whoever welcomes one such child in my name welcomes me."

MATTHEW 18:2-5

Opening Thoughts

My dad is a pastor, which means I grew up as a preacher's kid. Dad has always been a very passionate person, and that passion wasn't just contained in the pulpit. It also spilled out when he attended his kids' sporting events. He would tend to forget his pastoral persona and become "that parent"—the one who stood, yelled, and screamed as if he were the coach, not just a spectator.

There is one basketball game that stands out in particular in my memory. I was in junior high at the time, and I was having a terrible game. Besides missing most of my shots, I was one foul away from fouling out. The worse I played, the darker my dad's face became. I could tell this wasn't going to end well.

Then the inevitable happened. I jumped to block a shot and got called for a foul. The ref signaled for me to leave the court. As I headed to the bench, I heard a familiar voice yell from the stands. "Ref! Are you blind? That wasn't a foul. What are you talking about? That was a horrible call!"

Dad is an old-school preacher, and if there's one thing he knows how to do, it's project his voice. Trust me, his voice will stop you in your tracks and burn a hole in your soul. The entire crowd hushed, and all eyes turned toward my dad.

Then it got worse. In that small town, everyone knew my dad. Including the ref.

"Preacher!" The ref's voice reverberated through the stands. Apparently, he knew how to project, too. "That's it! You're outta here!" My dad—Reverend Wilkerson, a pastor, a man of God—was ejected from the game.

In retrospect it was rather awesome, but in the moment, I was mortified. I remember wondering, *Why does my dad care this much about winning?*

I think I know the answer. We *all* care about winning. We might not care about sports, but we have an inborn and God-given desire for greatness. I'm not talking about pride or egotism either. I'm talking about fulfilling our potential, about making our lives count, about living a life that leaves a legacy.

Jesus addressed this desire for greatness with his disciples in Mark 9. Prior to his comments, his disciples had been bickering about who was the greatest. Jesus didn't criticize their *desire* for greatness; rather, he clarified their *definition* of greatness. And he showed them how to achieve it.

He said, "Whoever wants to be first must take last place and be the servant of everyone else" (verse 35 NLT). In other words, the path to greatness is through service. We aren't great because we achieve influence, gain followers, and receive acclaim. We are great because we serve.

I think that Jesus could tell his disciples needed further explanation, so he pulled a child into the circle and held him in his arms. Then Jesus said, "Anyone who welcomes a little child like this on my behalf welcomes me, and anyone who welcomes me welcomes not only me but also my Father who sent me" (verse 37 NLT).

What was Jesus saying? To *welcome* someone has the idea of honoring, valuing, serving, and caring for someone. In that culture, children would have been seen as insignificant. They had no value and no voice. Children can't repay those who serve them. They can't earn their keep. Often, they don't even recognize or appreciate what they are given. And yet, Jesus told his disciples that welcoming a child is like welcoming him.

The meaning for us is clear. The path to greatness is the path of service, and the objects of that service are those who least deserve it, those who might not even appreciate it or value it. Truly great people love freely, without conditions and without expecting anything in return.

Jesus was the ultimate example of this kind of generous, selfless service. He made himself the friend of outcasts and sinners. He sought out those who could never repay his love. He gave his life for humanity, even though many of those humans were the ones who rejected, accused, and killed him.

Now, he asks us to use our lives to help people in need. That is our calling and our privilege. That is the path to greatness.

Video Teaching Notes

Here are a few key points to note as you watch this week's video. Use the space provided to write down any observations or applications that come to mind as you watch.

We all want to win. We all want to be great deep inside. We were designed for greatness by greatness.

Jesus saves us and transforms us, but he also calls us. He gives us purpose.

In Mark 9, Jesus gave his disciples a pathway to greatness. He said whoever wants to be first should become last.

We often have the wrong definition of greatness. We think it means to be known or to be better than everyone else. But that can never satisfy our soul.

How can last place become first place? When we change directions. That's the paradox of following Jesus: The way up is down. To receive we must give. To be first we must be last.

We can all be great because we can all serve. If we are too big to serve, we are too small to lead.

Our mission is to serve, just like one would serve a child: without expecting anything in return. Jesus came to serve, not to be served.

Jesus calls Judas "friend" even though he knew Judas was betraying him. That's who Jesus is. Even when we are far from him or fail him, he still pursues us, and he still has purpose for us.

Group Discussion Questions

Take a few minutes with your group members to discuss what you just watched and explore these concepts in Scripture.

1. What does the sentence "we were designed for greatness by greatness" mean to you?

2. What wrong concepts or definitions of greatness do some people have?

3. What was the pathway to greatness that Jesus gave his disciples?

4. How is this different than the pathway that our culture typically promotes?

5. We are called to be a "help desk" for people. Why do we sometimes *not* help those who look to us?

6. Why is it significant that Jesus called Judas Iscariot "friend"? What does that tell you about Jesus' attitude toward people?

Closing Prayer

Close your time together in prayer. Here are a few ideas of what you could pray about based on the topic of this session:

- Thank God for his unconditional love toward you, even when you didn't know him.
- Thank him for creating you and calling you toward true greatness.
- Pray that God would replace any selfishness or insecurity you have with humility, love, and true generosity.
- Ask God to help you know how to serve those around you better.
- Pray for grace to love those who mistreat you, accuse you, or harm you.

Recommended Reading

Review chapter 10 and the epilogue in the book *Friend of Sinners*. Use the space provided to write down any key points or questions that you might want to share with your group leader or group members in the upcoming weeks after the study is concluded.

PERSONAL STUDY

The following pages provide an opportunity for you to reflect personally on the topics you covered this week in the *Friend of Sinners* video and discussion. Feel free to engage with any or all of these three activities during the week. There are no right or wrong answers, and no one will see your responses unless you choose to share them. These moments alone with God are a time to allow his love, peace, and wisdom to fill your heart and mind.

The Path to Greatness

Jesus' disciples were typical human beings—concerned with *rights*, *recognition*, and *ranking*. But when Jesus asked them about their conversation, they didn't have the nerve to tell him what they were arguing about. Why? Because they knew it was petty and superficial. The funny thing is, we often do the same thing. We know we shouldn't be concerned with artificial, subjective things like fame and power. And yet, we all too easily find ourselves sucked into traps of comparison and competition. Jesus' words to his disciples are just as true today as they were back then. Take a few moments to evaluate your own journey toward greatness by answering the following questions.

Rights

"You have heard the law that says the punishment must match the injury: 'An eye for an eye, and a tooth for a tooth.' But I say, do not resist an evil person! If someone slaps you on the right cheek, offer the

other cheek also. If you are sued in court and your shirt is taken from you, give your coat, too. If a soldier demands that you carry his gear for a mile, carry it two miles. Give to those who ask, and don't turn away from those who want to borrow" (Matthew 5:38–42 NLT).

1. What "rights" do you consider especially important? (For example: the right to justice, the right to be heard, the right to be understood, the right to make up your own mind, or the right to defend yourself.)

2. How do you tend to react if those rights or expectations are violated?

3. How would taking on the attitude of a servant affect your reactions when your rights are infringed?

4. Is there ever a time to stand up for yourself when rights are violated? Can you still love and serve others while being a strong leader or an advocate for justice?

Recognition

"Watch out! Don't do your good deeds publicly, to be admired by others, for you will lose the reward from your Father in heaven. When you give to someone in need, don't do as the hypocrites do—blowing trumpets in the synagogues and streets to call attention to their acts of charity! I tell you the truth, they have received all the reward they will ever get. But when you give to someone in need, don't let your left hand know what your right hand is doing. Give your gifts in private, and your Father, who sees everything, will reward you" (Matthew 6:1–4 NLT).

1. Jesus said that we are to give and serve in secret. Why do you think he wants us to be okay with anonymity? How easy is it for you to serve without recognition, recompense, or gratitude?

2. How is serving an antidote for the human tendency to pursue fame and status?

3. Which do you think brings greater fulfillment: service or recognition? Why?

Ranking

Is there any encouragement from belonging to Christ? Any comfort from his love? Any fellowship together in the Spirit? Are your hearts tender and compassionate? Then make me truly happy by agreeing wholeheartedly with each other, loving one another, and working together with one mind and purpose. Don't be selfish; don't try to impress others. Be humble, thinking of others as better than yourselves. Don't look out only for your own interests, but take an interest in others, too (Philippians 2:1–4 NLT).

1. Competition has its place, but when we begin to rank ourselves in order to feel better about ourselves or to prove our value, it becomes toxic very quickly. What

are some of the negative effects of comparison and competition?

2. Does God compare his children to one another? How does God see us? How should that affect our tendency to rank one another?

3. How does becoming a servant defuse the negative effects of ranking, comparison, and competition?

I find that focusing on Jesus keeps my ego in check. The disciples veered from that, and their arguing about greatness was ridiculous. It was then, and it is now. Striving and competing to be great in the eyes of others is pointless, because we have Jesus with us. We need to keep our eyes on him. His presence, his love, and his grace are far more important than our egos. . . . The greatness Jesus modeled puts our lives and desires in perspective.

—*FRIEND OF SINNERS,* PAGES 193–194

Called to Serve, Called to Greatness

We were created with a purpose, and that purpose is greatness. We each have a call on our lives to make a difference. That doesn't mean God wants us to fix everyone's problems, of course, but he has a specific role for us. God is giving us the desire, grace, and resources to carry out what he has planned for us. It's thus important to identify the things God has called us to accomplish in life, because as we serve in those areas, we will help others and also find fulfillment ourselves.

1. *"For God is working in you, giving you the desire and the power to do what pleases him"* (Philippians 2:13 NLT). What two things does God give us that help us obey him? Where have you noticed these two things at work in your own life?

2. Often, your *compassion* is a key to your calling. Think about the various needs you see in the news, in your local community, and among your family and friends. What specific needs usually stir your compassion the most? List a few of the things that tug at your heart and compel you to act.

3. Another indicator of God's calling is a strong desire or *passion* to see change. Don't discount or underestimate that inner voice telling you to act. It just might be God! What are you most passionate about doing with your life?

4. What talents, gifts, hobbies, and *abilities* do you have? List three or four, and then brainstorm some specific ways you could use those abilities to serve others.

5. Where have you seen the most *results* when you've stepped up to meet needs and fix problems? Are there areas where people have told you that you're particularly gifted or skilled? Explain.

6. You often won't know you're good at something until you try it. No matter how young or old you are, what you've accomplished, or how long you've followed Jesus, you can always try new things. What are some areas of service or ministry you've wondered about trying? Would you be willing to pick one and try it in the next three months?

We desire greatness because we were created for greatness. It's a God-given desire, not a sinful desire. It's inherent in humanity. . . . God put within us an impulse to be the best we can be and to achieve the most we can achieve. We were designed to reach our potential. We were created in the image of a God who is great, so it's logical to sense greatness within ourselves.

—*FRIEND OF SINNERS,* PAGE 194

Loving the Unlovable

Jesus was a friend of sinners, even when those sinners rejected him or hated him. Nowhere is that clearer than in his final interactions with Judas, the man who betrayed him and sent him to his death. Jesus knew exactly what was going to happen. He had predicted it, after all. And yet he called Judas *friend.* Talk about loving your enemies! From start to finish, Jesus was an example of unconditional love. As followers of Jesus, we have the same calling to give, serve, and love like Jesus.

1. In Matthew 5:43–48, Jesus states:

   "You have heard the law that says, 'Love your neighbor' and hate your enemy. But I say, love your enemies! Pray for those who persecute you! In that way, you will be acting as true children of your Father in heaven. For he gives his sunlight to both the evil and the good, and he sends rain on the just and the unjust alike. If you love only those who love you, what reward is there for that? Even corrupt tax collectors do that much. If you are kind only to your friends, how are you different from anyone else? Even pagans do that. But you are to be perfect, even as your Father in heaven is perfect" (NLT).

   Are there people in your life who are difficult to love? Why? How do you tend to react around them?

2. Jesus' concept of friendship is very different from our culture's definition, especially when it comes to dealing with friends who fail us or harm us. In light of Jesus' concept of friendship, how should you react in the following scenarios?

   When a friend criticizes you . . .

When a friend betrays you . . .

When a friend misunderstands you . . .

When a friend hurts you . . .

3. Can you think of a time someone else showed you under-served, unconditional love? How did that make you feel?

4. In 1 Corinthians 13:4–7, Paul writes:

> *Love is patient and kind; love does not envy or boast; it is*
> *not arrogant or rude. It does not insist on its own way; it is*
> *not irritable or resentful; it does not rejoice at wrongdoing,*
> *but rejoices with the truth. Love bears all things, believes*
> *all things, hopes all things, endures all things* (ESV).

Are any of the characteristics of love listed here difficult for you? Explain.

What are some specific ways you can better show love toward people in your world?

Racism and prejudice are hot topics today, and for good reason. We all know we shouldn't discriminate based on such superficial things as economic status, ethnic background, gender, or religion. The scary thing about these issues, however, is they are usually blind spots—we don't see the assumptions or memories that keep us from seeing people like Jesus does. We need God's help to truly love the world as he does. Take a few moments to pray for the following areas:

- Pray that God would help you remove from your heart and emotions *all* barriers to loving people.
- Ask him to let you see people as he sees them: lost children in need of the Father's love.
- Finally, pray that you would be able to do your part in helping lost and hurting people. Ask for open doors, for wisdom, and for courage to become uncomfortable for the sake of comforting others.

Jesus is in hot pursuit of your heart. He is chasing you. Nothing you could do could change his passion for you. By the same token, he is passionate about others. Even about the people we would tend to discount or disqualify. Jesus loves them, and he wants you and me to reach out to them. . . . He will never give up on us. He will never stop loving us. He is the friend of sinners, and when we accept his friendship, his love, and his grace, we become friends for all eternity.

—FRIEND OF SINNERS, PAGES 212, 214

CONCLUSION

Thank you for being willing to spend these last five weeks growing closer to Jesus! I trust his love is a greater reality to you than ever before.

This is only the beginning, of course. The more you get to know Jesus, the more you realize how deep and high and far and wide his love extends. You will spend the rest of your life discovering his love, learning to trust him, and understanding his plan for you. It's a beautiful journey with the best friend you could ever imagine.

Along the way, though, there might be a few unexpected detours and roadblocks. Sometimes it's easy to sense God's love when you are curled up in a chair with a coffee and your Bible, but it's a lot harder when your boss is threatening to fire you or your marriage is struggling.

If I could encourage you with one thing, it would be this: *when times are tough, you need a friend the most.* Not a judge, not a condemner, not an accuser, not a boss. You need a friend, and that friend is Jesus. Don't allow your weaknesses or the stress of life to make you forget how passionate Jesus is about you. Instead, let those difficult times push you toward his love.

I am excited for the journey ahead of you! I know God has you on his mind and in his arms. Learn to lean on the friend of sinners, let him lead your life, and you'll never regret it.

—Rich Wilkerson, Jr.

LEADER'S GUIDE

Thank you so much for taking on the responsibility of leading or hosting this small-group study. You are amazing! Your investment in the lives of others is going to bear more fruit than you might imagine. Whether this is your first time leading a group or you've led groups like this before, below are a few suggestions to make the experience more effective and fun.

If you haven't done so already, take a few moments to read the "Introduction" and "How to Use This Guide" sections at the beginning of this study guide. Then peruse the various sections of the guide, especially the ones that pertain to the group sessions, so you get a feel for the layout and structure of the material. Below is a description of a recommended format for a small group, but there is no right or wrong way to use the study guide—it exists to benefit the group, and you as the leader are free to decide how best to utilize it.

What Is Your Role?

Your main role as a leader or host is to organize and run the weekly video discussions. That includes managing behind-the-scenes administrative details, providing a comforting and nurturing environment, facilitating the group discussion, and of course praying for those who attend. If your group is meeting as part of a small group or Sunday school ministry of your local church, you might have additional responsibilities such as following up with group members who have questions or needs during the week or reporting group attendance.

During the group sessions, don't feel obligated to answer all the questions, reteach the video content, or add a lot to it. Your function is primarily that of moderator or question-asker. Obviously, you can say whatever you need to say to lead the group, but don't feel like you have to be an expert or a master teacher in order to lead. The videos provide the core of the study, and the small group should be a mutually taught environment, where people learn not only from the videos but also from the discussion among the participants.

Encourage everyone in your group to get a copy of the study guide. Some of them might not read the introductory material in the guide, so at the first meeting, you should cover briefly the purpose of the study guide, especially the between-sessions activities. Reassure them the guide is a place where they can write down their honest answers and thoughts. They won't have to share anything publicly that they don't want to.

What Is the Best Environment for the Group?

The most important thing is not to have every detail worked out perfectly or have a totally polished presentation but rather to create an environment conducive to learning and authentic discussion. Do your best to plan ahead, of course, but don't stress out if things go wrong. It's almost inevitable! You might have trouble with the video, or the person in charge of snacks might not show up, or you might get stuck in traffic and arrive late to your own meeting. But at the end of the day, if the group has a good conversation and grows closer to God, it was a success!

Regarding a place to meet, if you have options other than a church sanctuary or formal classroom to host your small group, that is usually ideal. A home tends to inspire a more intimate and friendly environment than a church or classroom, and it is more disarming for first-time visitors. If you are meeting in an academic or religious setting, however, you can brainstorm ways to create an informal feel. Things like coffee and background music always help.

Make sure there is enough comfortable seating for everyone. It's always a good idea to plan for a few more than will probably come, but that doesn't mean you have to put out all the chairs right from the start. A room that feels empty can be a bit intimidating for people. When possible, a semicircle is usually the best set up. This allows for everyone to view the video while also keeping the discussion time natural and welcoming.

In most cases the leader should be the first one at the meeting, so plan on arriving at least twenty minutes before it is supposed to begin. That gives you time to arrange the chairs as well as set up (and test!) the video. It's much easier to be a welcoming, relaxed leader when you aren't struggling with forgotten details at the last second.

Greet participants as they arrive, hug and laugh with them, and get everyone talking. Introduce new people to friends you trust so that no one is alone. Snacks are always a great icebreaker that help produce a less-formal environment. You can provide snacks yourself or pass around a snack sign-up sheet during the first meeting.

Finally, if people in your group have small children (or if you know other people would come if childcare were available), consider organizing something for kids. It's a bit of work, but it can make all the difference for young families. If you do provide childcare, please remember how important it is to ensure the safety of the children by providing a safe area and responsible, trusted volunteers.

What Format Should the Group Sessions Follow?

Again, the exact format and schedule of the group sessions are up to you as the leader. Here is a recommended format, however, if you need a place to start.

Welcome and Prayer

Once people have arrived and have had a few minutes to just hang out and get to know each other, begin the study by welcoming everyone. It's often good to start a few minutes after the official start time, depending on the makeup of your group.

If you'd like, you can cheerfully remind people to silence their phones. Most parents will need their phones on them in case there is an emergency with their kids, but no one will mind a gentle suggestion to put their phones on silent. Along those lines, though, it's best to keep as few "rules" as possible. The last thing you want is for people to perceive a legalistic or condescending attitude.

After your welcoming comments, start the meeting with prayer. You or someone you know well can lead in a simple prayer thanking God for his love and asking him to open people's hearts and minds. If you'd like, prior to the prayer, you might ask if anyone has any specific needs or praise reports that they'd like to mention.

Video and Discussion

After prayer, introduce the topic for the week. Start by reading or summarizing the section titled "Opening Thoughts," which introduces the main ideas of the video. Don't start a discussion yet, just play the video. You might want to remind people that there are video teaching notes in their study guide with spaces to jot down further thoughts as they watch.

Once the video is over (they are between fifteen and twenty minutes long), turn off the television or screen and invite people to follow along with the discussion questions. You might choose to ask all the questions or just a few, depending on time. Don't be afraid of silence when you ask a question. If you immediately answer your own question, no one else will speak up. But if you give people a few moments to think, someone inevitably breaks the silence.

Try to get everyone involved in the discussion, but make sure that if someone does not feel comfortable enough to share, they don't feel obligated to do so. Find a balance between nudging people out of their comfort zones and providing a warm, accepting environment for all participants. As people share, you might want to expand on certain comments with follow-up questions such as "Why do you feel that way?" or "Can you tell us more about that?"

As the group host, you also have the responsibility of maintaining a healthy, safe environment. Without being rude, don't allow any one person (including yourself!) to dominate the group time. Be alert for participants who verbally attack those who don't agree with them or who consistently try to fix other people's problems uninvited. If participants are afraid of being attacked or shamed, they won't open up and share.

Remember, people don't always need answers, so don't worry if you don't have them. People need acceptance, and people need Jesus. You can give them both. Just point people to God and show them love. If you feel the conversation is veering too far off topic or into areas you aren't qualified to address, simply move on to the next question. It's okay for people to agree to disagree or to table a discussion for another time. If you need a question answered, you can seek counsel during the week from your pastor or another trusted advisor.

Finally, be aware of the time and respect people's schedules, especially if you are meeting on a weeknight and they have school-age children. If conversation or ministry is still going strong but you are out of time, consider officially dismissing the meeting but inviting anyone who so desires to stay longer.

Conclusion

End in prayer, using the "Closing Prayer" section notes if you'd like. Thank everyone for coming and remind them when and where the next meeting is, along with any other necessary details (such as who is bringing snacks next week). You can also reference the between-sessions activities for those who would like to dig deeper into the week's topic.

Again, thank you for your willingness to lead a group! It is one of the most rewarding and effective ways to serve others, and God will give you the grace, wisdom, and strength you need to be successful. And don't be surprised if you end up being the one who is most benefited by the group—after all, Jesus said it is more blessed to give than to receive. God has a way of pouring out his blessings on those who give their time and resources to help others. Enjoy the next few weeks!

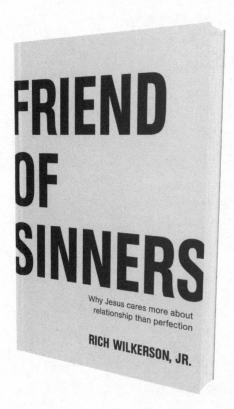